The Ghost Train

Maverick
Chapter Readers

'The Ghost Train'
An original concept by Cath Jones
© Cath Jones 2022

Illustrated by Katie Kear

Published by MAVERICK ARTS PUBLISHING LTD
Studio 11, City Business Centre, 6 Brighton Road,
Horsham, West Sussex, RH13 5BB
© Maverick Arts Publishing Limited May 2022
+44 (0)1403 256941

A CIP catalogue record for this book is available at the British Library.

ISBN 978-1-84886-882-3

www.maverickbooks.co.uk

This book is rated as: Lime Band (Guided Reading)

The Ghost Train

Written by
Cath Jones

Illustrated by
Katie Kear

Chapter 1

Dan let out a whoop of delight. He stared up in amazement at the Old Station House. Their new home was even better than he'd imagined!

"What do you think?" Mum asked.

"It's awesome!" he shouted. "I can't believe we're going to live in an abandoned railway station!"

She smiled. "Do you want to explore while I unload the van?"

Dan unlocked the front door. His heart thumped with excitement. Cobwebs dangled from the ceilings and everything was caked in dust. An old photograph album lay open on top of

a pile of boxes. It was full of black and white pictures of steam trains. Dan gazed at a photograph of a curly-haired man with sparkling eyes. Somehow he seemed familiar.

"What have you got there?" Mum asked curiously.

"Just old photographs…"

"That man looks just like you!" Mum gasped.

Dan froze. She was right!

"Do you think we're related?" he asked thoughtfully.

"It's possible… We Blackthorns originally came from this area. And of course this was your great-great-grandad's house…"

Dan carefully put the picture into his pocket.

That night, Dan lay in bed, imagining old steam trains waiting at the station.

Suddenly, his bedroom filled with a mysterious green glow. Dan gazed out of his window. An ancient train signal had flickered into life! An eerie mist slid over the station.

Toot toot!

He gaped in astonishment as a ghostly-looking steam train chugged past. The driver waved!

Every night, for the next two weeks, the same thing happened. The signal glowed green, and the ghostly train whizzed past. The driver waved and Dan waved back.

Then, one day, Dan found a battered-looking train timetable inside an old wardrobe. With a thrill of excitement, he realised a train was due to stop at the station at 11 o'clock that night. As he turned the timetable pages, a little piece of pink paper fluttered out.

He picked it up and examined it curiously. It was a return train ticket to the Station Hotel. Quickly, he checked the ancient-looking train timetable. Yes! The train stopping later that night was going to the Station Hotel. Excitement bubbled up inside him as he tucked the ticket into his pyjama pocket.

He set his alarm clock and closed his eyes. As sleep slipped over him, he wondered who would be on the train...?

BEEP-BEEP-BEEP.

Dan woke with a start. His bedroom glowed with a warm, red light. The train signal had turned red! But would the ghost train really stop?

Chapter 2

Dan raced down the stairs and crept onto the platform. The train tracks began to vibrate. Moments later, a shiny, dark green steam train slid out of the mist and screeched to a halt.

A door flew open and an odd-looking, young girl stepped out. She wore a bright red, flowing skirt and a sparkly, gold waistcoat. Dan gazed with big, shocked eyes.

Her face was so pale he could see almost right through her!

"Welcome to the Ghost Train!" she said.

Dan stared speechlessly.

"Hurry up and climb aboard! We've got a timetable to keep to," she said.

Without warning, the train shuddered into motion. Dan only just had time to leap aboard.

"It's rude to stare," said the girl. "Haven't you seen a ghost before?"

"You're my first!" Dan whispered weakly.

"Well then, I'm Bessie Le Fleur. Magician *extraordinaire* at your service."

She gave a little bow and produced a pack of cards.

"A magician!" Dan gasped.

"Have you got your train ticket?" she asked. "The ticket inspector will want to see it."

Dan nodded and began to rummage in his pocket. The photograph of the curly-haired man fluttered to the floor.

Bessie picked it up. "Why have you got a picture of Embers?" she asked.

"Embers?" Dan repeated.

She nodded. "You look a bit like him!" she said curiously.

"I think we might be related." His voice trembled with excitement.

"Sometimes he drives the train," she said. "We can go and find him if—"

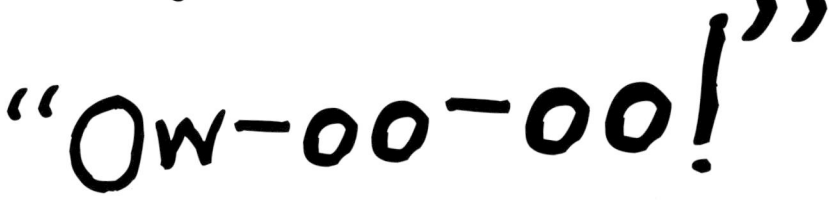

"Ow-oo-oo!"

A horrifying howl cut across Bessie's words.

Dan spun round in terror.

Chapter 3

"No need to look so scared. Follow me!" Bessie laughed and opened the door to the next carriage.

"Aahhhhhhhh!"

Dan let out a blood-curdling scream.

Six terrifying-looking ghosts stared at him.

Some floated beneath the ceiling, others hovered above the floor.

"Whooo-aaaah!"

Bessie gave a spine-chilling moan.

All the ghosts clapped.

"Bravo, Bessie. First-class moan," said a spidery-looking woman. She waved at Dan. "Welcome to Ghost School."

Dan gaped in surprise. "Ghost School?"

The woman nodded.

"G-g-g-ghosts go to school?" Dan stammered.

"Of course; you don't just die and instantly know how to be a ghost," the teacher said. "You have to *learn* how to be scary: how to hover, how to moan…"

"Sorry, miss!" Bessie interrupted. "We don't have time for lessons today. We're looking for Embers."

Dan held out the photograph. "I think we're related."

"I saw Embers earlier, in another carriage," said a ghost with a handbag. "He was still getting ready though."

"Getting ready for what?" Dan asked.

"The party!" the teacher replied. "You should come! But make sure you catch the return train, otherwise we'll be seeing a lot more of you at Ghost School!"

Wait, what?! Dan thought. *Does that mean I would turn into a ghost?* But before Dan could reply, there was a loud screeching of brakes.

"We've arrived!" exclaimed Bessie.

Chapter 4

Bessie's eyes sparkled with excitement. "Ta dah!" She pointed at an enormous building towering over the platform.

"The Station Hotel," read Dan. "So is this where the party is?"

"Yes! And that's not all…" Bessie grinned and shuffled her pack of cards. She flipped the cards so fast from one hand to the other, that Dan was sure she would drop them. He'd never seen anyone shuffle a pack of cards so fast! Then, she threw them all into the air. For a moment, the cards floated above Dan's head. She waved her hands mysteriously and the cards formed into the shape of a cake complete with candles.

"A birthday cake!" Dan exclaimed.

Bessie shook her head. "Not *birth*day, *death*day. It's when we celebrate the day someone became a ghost."

"Hurry up, you two! We're going to be late!" fussed the handbag ghost.

All the ghosts rushed to leave at once. Some passed straight through the wall of the train. Others floated out of the window. A few took the door.

"Of course! I can't believe I forgot. Tonight is *Embers's* deathday party!" Bessie exclaimed. "Come on!"

They hurried after the other ghosts. One by one, the ghosts stopped in front of a brick wall.

Then they walked *through* it!

"Now you," said Bessie.

"But I'm not a ghost. I can't pass through a wall!" Dan objected.

"It's the only way into Embers's deathday party…"

Dan ran his hand over the wall. He wanted to meet Embers but…

"Hold my hand and we'll walk through together," Bessie whispered.

He held her ice-cold hand and closed his eyes. As she tugged him *into* the wall, his skin tingled. His fingers and toes seemed to burn with cold. When he opened his eyes, he was standing in the middle of a dimly lit corridor.

Chapter 5

The sound of happy laughter drifted down the corridor. They turned a corner and Dan stopped in his tracks. Hundreds of ghosts filled a large room. There was a stage at the front with a huge deathday cake with lots of candles. A group of happy-looking ghosts gathered next to it.

Bessie zoomed across the room and onto the stage, floating above the crowd. "Embers!" she yelled.

A curly-haired ghost turned. It was the man from Dan's photograph!

"I've brought someone to meet you!" Bessie said.

"Blimey!" He stared at Dan. "Don't we look alike?!"

Dan held out the photograph. "I found this in the station house. Mum inherited the house from her great-grandad and we've just moved in."

Embers looked thoughtful. "Do you know your great-great-grandad's name?"

"Samuel Blackthorn," said Dan.

Bessie gasped. "Embers! Isn't that your name?"

Embers nodded. "Dan, I think you must be my great-great-grandson!" He held out his hand. "Samuel Blackthorn at your service."

Before Dan could reply, a band suddenly started to play loud music.

Bessie bobbed into the air and whirled round. "Let's dance!"

The three of them hopped and spun together.

Whenever the music stopped, Embers told Dan more about the Blackthorn family and Bessie performed card tricks. Dan watched with wide eyes as she threw the whole pack of cards into the air and made one card stick to the ceiling!

Everyone cheered when Embers managed to blow out all one hundred candles on his deathday cake.

Dan was just thinking that this was definitely the best party he'd ever been to, even if the cake had tasted rather odd, when there was the sound of a distant whistle.

"The train!" gasped Dan. He'd been having such a brilliant time he'd completely forgotten about returning home.

Ghosts sped from the room.

"Hurry!" yelled Bessie.

Dan gulped. He couldn't miss the train!

Dan, Bessie and Embers raced towards the platform. The train was already speeding up! They were too late…

Suddenly, a train door flew open and a hand reached out.

Chapter 6

Dan grabbed the outstretched hand. Wind whipped at his clothes as he was pulled through the open door of the train.

"Thanks!" he gasped. He'd made it. He wasn't going to turn into a ghost!

Bessie whizzed into the carriage, closely followed by Embers. Dan grinned at them.

"That was close!" laughed Embers.

A uniformed man held open the door, as more and more ghosts flew on board. Finally, he slammed it shut. "Same every time," he muttered. "Ghosts are terrible time keepers!"

"Apart from you!" teased Bessie. "Dan, this is the ticket inspector."

Dan plunged his hand into his pocket to get his train ticket. But the pocket was empty! The ticket inspector fixed Dan with a hard stare.

"Ticket?" he asked, raising one eyebrow questioningly. Dan gulped nervously.

"Come on, inspector," said Embers, "let my great-great-grandson off just this once!"

"Hmm." The inspector raised an eyebrow again. Then he smiled. "Well, lucky for you, I happen to have a spare ticket here." He gave Dan a ticket.

"That's my lost ticket!" Dan gasped, relieved.

"That's even luckier then!" the inspector laughed.

Dan, Bessie and Embers settled in a carriage together. Bessie taught Dan card tricks and Embers told him funny family stories. The train journey flew by.

Finally, Embers said, "It's your stop soon, Dan."

Reluctantly, Dan stood up. He wasn't ready to say goodbye yet.

"Next time, we'll perform card tricks on stage together," Bessie announced.

"That'd be brilliant!" said Dan. "Only…" his voice trailed off. "I don't know when I'll be back."

Chapter 7

The train pulled into Dan's station and he climbed down onto the platform. Dozens of ghosts floated out behind him.

"Goodbye, Dan!"

"Take care, Dan."

"See you soon, Dan!"

Everyone had come to say goodbye.

Embers drifted over. "I thought I might hang around and haunt the station house!" He chuckled and gazed around with a dreamy expression.

Toot toot!

A whistle blew. Suddenly, Dan felt overwhelmed with emotion. Embers was staying and Dan had made so many friends...

"Dan!" yelled Bessie. "Catch!"

A pack of playing cards bobbed through the air. He reached up and grabbed them.

"Don't forget to practise our tricks," she laughed.

Dan shuffled the cards. "I promise I'll practise every day! Maybe you can visit?" he asked hesitantly.

But before Bessie could answer, the ticket inspector appeared. "Just a moment, lad."

Dan waited nervously as the crowd of ghosts parted for the inspector.

"I forgot to give you this." He held out a ticket.

"A souvenir?" Dan asked with a puzzled expression.

"A ticket for your next journey aboard the ghost train!"

"Thank you!" Dan gasped.

"All aboard!" yelled the inspector. Steam hissed from the engine and the wheels began to turn.

"See you soon, Dan," cried Bessie.

Dan waved and waved until Bessie and the train vanished into a tunnel.

With a happy sigh, he followed Embers into the house. He climbed into bed and closed his eyes. "Goodnight, Embers," he whispered as sleep washed over him.

★★★

"Dan! Wake up, sleepy head!" said a faint voice.

44

He stared around sleepily. What was happening? Where was he?

Mum squeezed his shoulder. "You look exhausted. Didn't you sleep well?"

Dan grinned sheepishly.

Mum rubbed the sleeve of his pyjamas. "What *have* you been up to? You're covered in soot!"

Embers winked at Dan as he floated round the room, behind Mum's back.

Discussion Points

1. What did Dan find in the beginning?

2. What happened when the train signal turned red?

a) The Ghost Train kept going
b) The Ghost Train stopped
c) Dan made a wish

3. What was your favourite part of the story?

4. Who carries a pack of cards?

5. Why do you think Dan was able to go through the wall at the Station Hotel when he isn't a ghost?

6. Who was your favourite character and why?

7. There were moments in the story when Dan experienced **new things**. Where do you think the story shows this most?

8. What do you think happens after the end of the story?

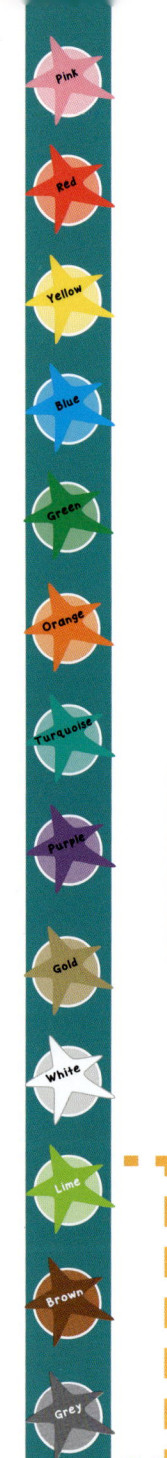

Book Bands for Guided Reading

The Institute of Education book banding system is a scale of colours that reflects the various levels of reading difficulty. The bands are assigned by taking into account the content, the language style, the layout and phonics. Word, phrase and sentence level work is also taken into consideration.

The Maverick Readers Scheme is a bright, attractive range of books covering the pink to grey bands. All of these books have been book banded for guided reading to the industry standard and edited by a leading educational consultant.

To view the whole Maverick Readers scheme, visit our website at www.maverickearlyreaders.com

Or scan the QR code to view our scheme instantly!

Maverick Chapter Readers
(From Lime to Grey Band)

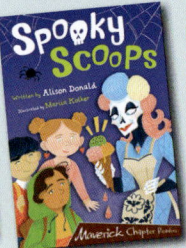